THE TRAP

Kieran Lynn

THE TRAP

OBERON BOOKS
LONDON

WWW.OBERONBOOKS.COM

First published in 2017 by Oberon Books Ltd
521 Caledonian Road, London N7 9RH
Tel: +44 (0) 20 7607 3637 / Fax: +44 (0) 20 7607 3629
e-mail: info@oberonbooks.com
www.oberonbooks.com

A catalogue record for this book is available from the British
Library.

PB ISBN: 9781786823106
E ISBN: 9781786823113

Cover artwork by Fraser Gillespie | www.fgillespie.co.uk

Characters

Tom – An employee

Clem – An employee

Alan – A branch manager

Meryl – A regional manager

SCENE ONE

Midnight. The office/shop of Debt Duck, a payday loan company. The walls are covered with promotional material for the company that showcases its cartoon-ish brand mascot, the Debt Duck.

The sound of keys jangling is heard and the front door opens. A figure dressed in black runs into the room and leaps over one of the desks. A moment later, TOM enters, in ordinary clothes and clutching a large bunch of keys.

On the wall is an alarm panel. The alarm speaks in the typical computer voice.

ALARM: Door opened. Please enter your code now.

TOM enters a code.

ALARM: Code accepted. The alarm has been deactivated. Thank you

TOM turns into the room.

TOM: There are so many keys on here. Too many really. We should think about labeling them.

TOM turns into the room.

TOM: Clem? Clem, where are you?

He walks into room, but it's dark and he trips over a chair.

TOM: Ow!

He stands up and turns the lights on.

CLEM: Turn off the lights!

TOM: Sorry.

TOM does.

CLEM: We're knocking the joint off, Tom! You don't turn on the big lights when you're knocking a joint off.

TOM: I'm sorry. I've never done this before.

CLEM: I would have thought that was obvious.

TOM: I couldn't see you. I'm sorry.

CLEM: Let's just get on with it. So, Phase One is complete. Enter the building, undetected. Now, Phase Two.

CLEM takes a list out of her pocket.

TOM: You made a list?

CLEM: A plan, Tom. I made a plan.

TOM: Let me see.

TOM takes the list.

TOM: Phase One: Enter the building. Phase Two: Secure the scene. Phase Three: Crack the safe. Phase Four: Take the… loot. What are we Clem, pirates?

CLEM: I didn't know what else to call it.

TOM: Phase Five: Cover our tracks.

CLEM: And Phase Six: The getaway.

TOM: Look at this, you've even subcategorized Phase Five: Cover our tracks. Close safe. Clean prints. Secure building.

CLEM: Listen Tom, when the shit hits the fan, who knows which way it's going to fly?

TOM: What does that mean?

CLEM: It means that operations like this are very different when they actually happen. Adrenaline can easily take over a man, or woman, when he, or she, is involved in a high stakes op like this. I'm not about to let that happen, so I've made a plan. And talking about the plan was not in the plan, so let's get back to business.

TOM: Okay.

CLEM: Good. Now, lock the door.

TOM moves to the door.

TOM: Why do we want to be locked in?

CLEM: Because then, if the police come to check out why the lights were turned on, they'll find the door locked, nothing out of the ordinary and they'll be on their way.

TOM: What makes you think the police are coming?

CLEM: The police aren't coming.

TOM: You just said they were.

CLEM: Yes, but I was being hypothetical.

TOM: What if someone saw me turning the lights on?

CLEM: They didn't.

TOM: How do you know?

CLEM: Well, obviously I don't know for sure, but they were on for a very short amount of time. What are the chances that someone saw them?

TOM: I'd say very high.

CLEM: Almost non-existent. We're just being extra cautious. Now, lock the door.

TOM: Okay.

TOM is trying to find the right key.

TOM: I never know which key it is!

CLEM: Tom, keep your voice down.

TOM: I'm sorry Clementine, I'm tense. I always raise my voice when I'm tense, you know that. Why did I turn the lights on? I think we should go.

CLEM: We're not going until we get what we came for.

TOM: ... I don't know, Clem.

CLEM: You don't know what?

TOM: I don't know if I want to do this anymore.

CLEM: Tom, we've already been through this.

TOM: I know we have.

CLEM: We went through it at your house, we went through it again as we were leaving your house, we went through it walking here, we went through it outside the door and now we're going through it again. This company has taken from us, and now we're going to take something from them.

TOM: By stealing though?

CLEM: It's only stealing if you get caught.

TOM: No, even if you don't get caught, it's still stealing.

CLEM: Tom, we're doing this. The way this company has treated us, this is exactly what it deserves. In fact, it probably deserves worse, stealing this money, on the scale of things, is actually quite generous. Now, let's get on with it.

TOM: I'm not sure, Clem. I'm having second thoughts.

CLEM: You've already had your second thoughts Tom, and your third thoughts, and fourth and fifth thoughts, pretty soon your thoughts are going to be in double figures. This really isn't a very big deal. I mean, you must have stolen from work before?

TOM: …

CLEM: Have you?

TOM: Clem, is this really important?

CLEM: You have! What did you take?

TOM: … When it was my mother's birthday and I bought her that statue, the one that you didn't like.

CLEM: It was an ugly statue, Tom.

TOM: Well, I forgot to buy Sellotape to wrap it. So, I took a roll home, and I never brought it back.

CLEM: See? There we go. You stole a roll of Sellotape to wrap up a hideous statue.

TOM: It was nice.

CLEM: But you don't lie awake at night, wracked with guilt at the theft of that Sellotape, do you? Now, all you have to do is imagine that that Sellotape is a big pile of cash, and let's get on with it.

TOM: Well, I don't think anyone ever went to the electric chair for stealing Sellotape.

CLEM: Nobody ever went to the chair for stealing money either. You'd get a couple of months in prison at the absolute worst.

TOM: Is this supposed to be making me feel better?

CLEM: And we haven't even mentioned how it got this money in the first place.

TOM: What difference does that make?

CLEM: It's usury, Tom, plain and simple. Dante had a whole circle of hell just for the moneylenders, and it was the seventh out of nine, so it's getting pretty hot by then. Of course, they shared it with the blasphemers and the sodomites, so I'm not saying that it wouldn't be a good party, but it makes a point.

TOM: And what is the point?

CLEM: What this business does is legal, but it is highly unethical. And stealing from it may be illegal, but, all things considered, it's highly ethical.

TOM: ... You're right.

CLEM: So?

TOM: Let's rip this bitch!

CLEM: Yes!

They celebrate their decision momentarily. Before TOM takes out the keys.

TOM: I'll just have to find which key it is. So many. Too many really. I should label them.

CLEM: Take your time.

TOM looks through the keys, CLEM sits at ALAN's desk. She begins looking in drawers of ALAN's desk. She takes out a magazine.

TOM: Clem, what are you doing?

CLEM: Don't worry, I'll clean off the prints in phase five subcategory three.

CLEM takes out a crumpled magazine.

CLEM: The Dog Days Magazine. *(Reading.)* "Will Sally Flash take the cup at Montgomery?" No idea what that means.

TOM: *(Talking to a key.)* I don't even know what this one is for.

She takes out a bottle of whisky.

CLEM: Well, hello.

TOM: And he criticizes me for taking a lunch break.

CLEM: Credit card bills. He's a big spender.

TOM: *(About the keys.)* Here it is.

CLEM: Bingo. Phase Three: Open the safe.

TOM opens the safe. It's full of cash.

TOM: Ten thousand, in cash.

CLEM: That's a lot of money.

TOM: I know.

CLEM: Just think what you could do with all of that. You could live out your wildest dreams.

TOM: I could pay my rent for a year.

CLEM: I could pay off my student loans.

TOM: ... Are they really our wildest dreams?

CLEM reaches into the safe.

TOM: We're taking two thousand. That's what we agreed. Two thousand, which I should be able to cover up with some creative accounting. Let's not get carried away and make a mistake now that we're here. Just like you said, we have to stick to the plan.

TOM takes out a plastic bag.

CLEM: A plastic bag? I know we're not exactly Bonnie and Clyde, but couldn't you have found something a bit more stylish?

CLEM begins putting the money into a plastic bag.

TOM: It's inconspicuous.

CLEM: Just make sure you recycle it when we're done. Those things wreak havoc with the oceans.

TOM hears something.

TOM: What's that noise?

The sound gets louder, it is keys jangling. CLEM moves towards the door.

CLEM: Someone is at the door.

TOM: What?

CLEM: Shut the safe. Shut it now!

They spring into action. Locking the safe, putting stuff back in the desk drawers etc.

TOM: What do we do?

CLEM: Hide!

They both duck behind TOM's desk, just as the door opens. ALAN, looking very disheveled, enters. He turns on the lights and moves to the alarm panel. It takes him a moment to realise it is not turned on.

ALAN: That bastard forgot to turn on the alarm.

ALAN turns around and walks towards the safe. When he gets there he begins searching his pockets, before realizing that he doesn't have the keys.

ALAN: And he's got the keys to the safe.

He places his hands on his desk. Takes a deep breath. Then he has a fit of rage and tears up anything in sight. He shoves the contents of his desk to the floor. Kicks his chair. It is sudden and frightening.

As soon as it came it is gone. He breathes deeply. He takes the whisky from his drawer and takes several deep swigs. Before walking back to the alarm panel. He begins tapping away.

ALARM: Incorrect code entered.

ALAN: What?

He tries again.

ALARM: Incorrect code entered.

ALAN: I HATE YOU, YOU STUPID ALARM!

He thinks, before re-entering.

ALARM: Correct code entered.

ALAN: I'm sorry I shouted.

ALARM: Please reset your code.

He enters a different code.

ALARM: Thank you. Your code has been changed. The alarm will be activated in ten... Nine... Eight... Seven...

ALAN drinks the last of the whisky. He dumps the bottle in the bin.

ALARM: Six... Five...

ALAN exits, locking the door behind him. CLEM and TOM stand up, without the bag, and run to the door.

CLEM: We've got to get out of here now.

TOM: We can't he's still out there.

ALARM: Four... Three...

CLEM: The back door.

They run to the back of the shop.

TOM: Wait, where is the bag?

CLEM: Forget the bag.

TOM: I can't forget the bag!

ALARM: Two...

TOM grabs the bag from behind the desk and heads back towards CLEM.

ALARM: One. Alarm activated.

CLEM and TOM freeze in the middle of the room.

SCENE TWO

8:30am. Earlier that day. ALAN and MERYL.

MERYL: I didn't mean to upset you Alan, I really didn't.

ALAN: You told me I look liked like shit, Meryl.

MERYL: I said that because you look like shit, not because I wanted to upset you. Are you sure you're feeling okay?

ALAN: I'm fine. I'm fine. Really. Fine. I'm just... I'm fine.

MERYL: ... So, you're saying that you're fine?

ALAN: I wasn't expecting to see you standing outside the shop at half past eight in the morning. That's all. I wasn't prepared. Plus, I've just had a new alarm installed and it keeps going off in the middle of the night.

MERYL: Really?

ALAN: And I've tried to turn the sensitivity down, but the thing is like an Enigma machine. Every time I try to do something I end up doing something else. I tried to change the code this morning and ended up calling the Fire Brigade. Anyway, let's get down to business shall we?

MERYL: Straight shooting. I like that about you, Alan. You don't talk vegetables, you get straight to the meat.

ALAN: So, what is it?

MERYL: Well, in a nutshell, the earnings for your branch have consistently fallen short of our projections, so I'm here to tell you that you have one month to improve or we will terminate your employment.

ALAN: Big nutshell.

MERYL: Look Alan, I'm not going to rub your shoulders. I'm here to tell it like it is. We have an exceptionally accurate system for measuring what the earnings should be in each branch at any given time of year. It's quite amazing really. The predictability of human desperation is incredible. There are increases on Fridays, before national sporting occasions and a spike the size of Mount Everest in the run up to Christmas. It's beautiful. Sadly, your branch has failed repeatedly to live up to our expectation. Now, is that because our projections are wrong?

ALAN: Maybe.

MERYL: It's not. I assure you. The numbers don't lie. Now, do you want to tell me what's going on?

ALAN: … I don't know. I mean… I certainly… It feels like we're doing pretty well.

MERYL: Well, something is going wrong somewhere and now is not the time to be bad at this. As you know, the government is expected to announce new regulations for the short term lending industry. We don't know yet exactly how severe the regulations will be, so we're trying to get prepared before they are announced.

ALAN: Right. I see. And are these regulations likely to have a big impact on the business?

MERYL: Difficult to say... The government wants to look like they're improving our financial system, but they also quite like our financial system, so they'll probably leave the big boys untouched and come after us.

ALAN: Let's hope not.

MERYL: Let's hope not indeed. We're a small, high street business. It makes a relatively small amount of money off a relatively small proportion of the population. That's nothing compared to what some of what goes on in the world of making money. Oh, I get it, we're moneylenders. It's usury, it's in the Bible and Shakespeare, but what about derivatives or mortgage backed securities? Just because there isn't a commandment about credit default swaps they get away with it. We have a simple product and we're an easy target for simple minds. Anyway, I might as well level with you here Alan, there is an outside chance that these regulations could be very, very hard on us. I was talking to our owner last night.

ALAN: To Trevor Wynyard?

MERYL: Trevor and I were discussing the future of this business. He suggested that, in the worst case, there could be branch closures, cut backs, he even mentioned liquidating the company, but I'm pretty sure that was a joke.

ALAN: He would never do that.

MERYL: He would if it stopped him losing money. No, he was joking. Of course he was joking. Wynyard has promised that whatever happens his top people will be consulted.

ALAN: Does that include me?

MERYL: No. But it does include me, and then I can include you.

ALAN: Liquidating the company? What will I do if I lose my job?

MERYL: That's the spirit, Alan. Think of yourself.

ALAN: Sorry Meryl, I'm just processing this.

MERYL: Don't worry about the big boy stuff, Alan. It will be a set back, not a defeat. Trying to regulate capitalism is like trying to damn a river with tennis balls. The water will find a way to get through. People can rise up, they can demand more protection and they can petition the government for more regulation, they can have their little sit-ins and they can have their little marches, but rest assured Alan, that as long as the aim of the game is making money, we'll find a way to get it done.

ALAN: That makes me feel better.

MERYL: Personally, I can only imagine that they will do the absolute bare minimum, anyway.

ALAN: You think so?

MERYL: Oh, come on Alan. Don't be naïve. A government's primary role is to monitor the scales of satisfaction between the two basic elements of society – The rich and the rest of us. That's it. They stand in the middle and they make sure that the rich are happy and that the rest of us are happy enough not to notice how rich the rich are. I don't blame them. In fact, they probably don't even know that they're doing it half the time. The government is no longer the protector of the people, it's the protector of the economy. They don't care about you, me or any of us. They care about the markets and the indices and the companies and the currency. Those are their real constituents.

ALAN: I've never really looked at it like that before.

MERYL: Well, that's partially why it is the way it is. Anyway, we're off topic again. The reason I am here, is that, as we await the announcement of the new regulations, Wynyard wants to streamline the business and so we're trimming our sails a little bit.

ALAN: Meaning?

MERYL: We're making cuts.

ALAN: You're cutting my salary?

MERYL: Yes, but we don't call it that in the business world. We call it trimming your operating budget. It makes it easier for you to take. Wynyard is going to cut my salary unless I reduce the operating budgets of the branches in my region and I don't want my salary cut, so I'm going to pass it on to the branch managers and cut their salaries. I am sorry, but I bought a big house at the top of the market, and now I'm stuck with it Alan, really just stuck with it. I can't afford to let my mortgage get on top of me. I'm sorry.

ALAN: So, there's no negotiation? It's take it or leave it?

MERYL: I know, the powerlessness is enough to make you scream, but it's no one's fault. People get in tough times so they ask for more regulation and protection, the government provides more regulation, then businesses feel the squeeze, which they pass on to the people, then the people demand more regulation. It's a cycle that never ends, like the snake that eats its own shit.

ALAN: Tail.

MERYL: Either way, going forward we need to tighten up. That is going to mean increased reporting from all of our branches.

ALAN: What do you mean?

MERYL: Well, you'll be seeing a lot more of me, put it that way.

ALAN: That's not good.

MERYL: Why would you say that?

ALAN: ... Oh, no reason. Yes, increased reporting. Sounds like a good idea.

MERYL: We'll start next week. So, please look through your accounts and make sure everything is in order. Save yourself the headaches in the long run.

ALAN: Yes, this is bad.

MERYL: Again, that isn't really the response I was expecting.

ALAN: No, yes, just thinking of the workload I'm going to have today. That's all.

MERYL: I wouldn't worry about it, Alan. You'll turn things around. This branch is a gold mine. I mean look at your location. There are pubs, off-licenses, betting shops, pawn shops, cash for gold – it's the forest that grew from the ashes of crisis and it is fertile ground for us.

ALAN: I know.

MERYL: … I'm getting the sense you're feeling a little down about this, Alan.

ALAN: No. I'm really just fine.

MERYL: It's okay. You're not the only one. A big part of my job is making sure my managers keep their heads up. I know a lot of people say a lot of mean spirited things about us, and I know the toll that that can take.

ALAN: Really, I'm fine. I think this has all just been a lot to take in, that's all.

MERYL: You're an important part of society, Alan. Keep telling yourself that. Repeat it to yourself in the mirror, write it on a Post-it note and put it in your car, do whatever it takes but you have to start believing it. You are an important part of society.

ALAN: Do even you believe that?

MERYL: Do you think I'd be doing this if I hadn't forced myself to believe in it?

ALAN: … What?

MERYL: Imagine a girl, let's call her Jenny. Jenny is very nice, but has fallen upon hard times, lost her job, single mother, couple of kids, whatever. She has bills coming in and needs a little cash. She can't go to a bank, because she won't get approved. She can come to us, and get a short-term loan, which she can repay when her ship comes in. If we're not here, where does she go? Her bills don't go away, her need doesn't go away, but we have. So, she takes a trip to a loan shark, and before you know it her front door is getting kicked in, she's being threatened, and her possessions taken – who knows what else? We could have saved that girl from everything. You and me. We're their lifeboat, Alan. We pull them out of the shark-infested waters. Without us they get ripped apart and eaten whole.

ALAN: If they're ripped apart, then how are they eaten whole?

MERYL: I think you're focusing on the wrong part of the story. We're heroes, Alan. The amount of people we help we're practically a charity.

ALAN: I suppose… In a way… We are.

MERYL: That's a start. Remember Alan, we're just a shop. We sell a certain product at a certain price. We sell money and money is heavily in demand. So, customers are going to keep marching in here, and that's all they are, Alan, they're customers, the same as any other business. They march in here looking for a product and we've got it. So, you wrap it up in paper, slap it with a bow and sell it to them. That's it. Take comfort, Alan. We live in an age of buying and selling so why don't we take comfort that we're the sellers?

MERYL begins heading towards the door.

MERYL: … How many people work with you here?

ALAN: Two. Tom and Clementine.

MERYL: And who is your favourite?

ALAN: Oh, I don't know. Tom's been here longer.

MERYL: Then let's get rid of the other one.

ALAN: Sack her?

MERYL: Yes. You can do that, can't you?

ALAN: I'd rather not.

MERYL: I can do it, if you'd prefer?

ALAN: No. No, I'll do it. You just go and leave it to me. Leave everything to me.

MERYL: Okay. Well, I'll stop by again this afternoon.

ALAN: Oh, you really don't need to do that.

MERYL: Something tells me I do, Alan. Shall we say three o'clock? Perfect.

MERYL exits.

SCENE THREE

12:30am. TOM and CLEM are as they were at the end of scene one, frozen in the middle of the room.

CLEM: *(Without moving her mouth.)* Will it set the alarm off if I move my mouth?

TOM: What?

CLEM: Will…it…set…the…alarm…off…if… I…move…my… mouth?

TOM: I don't know what you're saying.

CLEM: Will…it…

TOM: Just talk Clementine, it won't set the alarm off if you move your mouth.

CLEM: This wasn't part of my plan. We're supposed to be onto Phase Four: Covering our tracks, by now.

22

TOM: Well, we've been diverted onto Phase: Our lives are over so let's just curl up in a ball on the floor and weep for our lost potential.

CLEM: ... That's not a real phase.

TOM: None of them were real phases! They were just some words that you wrote down on a piece of paper.

CLEM: Don't worry, Tom. I'll get us out of this. We just need to remain calm and think this through.

TOM: Okay. Let's think it through. We're inside the shop in the middle of the night, I'm holding a plastic bag full of stolen cash, and the slightest move either one of us makes will set off the alarm. Alan has changed the alarm code, so when it goes off I can't deactivate it. There is no way out of this.

CLEM: Crime always seems like such a good idea at the time.

TOM: Actually, it doesn't. In fact, if you think back, I said a million times that this was a terrible idea, because I knew that something like this would happen.

CLEM: A million is bit of an exaggeration. It was probably closer to six.

TOM: We're going to prison.

CLEM: No, we're not. We just stay like this until the morning. Then in the morning we move, the alarm goes off – You deactivate it and say it went off accidentally when you were opening up the shop. No one would question it, you work here. We put the money back in the safe, I'll slip out the back door and we'll carry on with our lives.

TOM: What time is it now?

CLEM: Must be about twelve-thirty.

TOM: So, we stay like this for the next seven and a half hours? Without moving a single muscle? Without going to the bathroom? Without sitting down, eating anything, or drinking anything?

CLEM: Do you think that is too long?

TOM: Of course I think it's too long. It is too long!

CLEM: I'm just working with what we have.

TOM: Just forget it, Clem. I can't believe I let you talk me into this.

CLEM: This is all Alan's fault.

TOM: It isn't Alan's fault. He doesn't make the decisions. He does what the company tells him to do.

CLEM: Then it's Trevor Wynyard's fault for making cuts.

TOM: He's just protecting himself and the business from government regulations.

CLEM: Then it is the government's fault.

TOM: They're just responding to what they think people want.

CLEM: Then it's the people's…no, it's not our fault! I don't want the entire world Tom, I just want to have thoughts that aren't all about money.

TOM: I know. Me too.

CLEM: It should be a right, shouldn't it? I hate this feeling. I feel like I'm going to spend my entire life just making ends meet. I'll live someone else's life because I couldn't afford my own.

TOM: I know. I feel like we're well and truly stuck.

CLEM: Well, I don't want to point out the obvious Tom, but…

TOM: Very funny.

CLEM: Anyway, I doubt anything we can do will make any difference. So, let's get on with it.

TOM: Get on with what?

CLEM: New plan. Plan B. Phase One: Set off the alarm.

TOM: Why would we want to do that?

CLEM: Phase Two: Return the loot to the safe.

TOM: I asked you not to call it loot.

CLEM: Phase Three: Wait outside until Alan and/or the police arrive.

TOM: We wait for them to arrive?

CLEM: Phase Four: Claim innocence.

TOM: How does that work?

CLEM: We explain that the alarm went off during the night. We arrived, which is part of your job, but you couldn't deactivate it. Then, Alan will realize that we couldn't deactivate it because he changed the code. No one has broken in and nothing is missing from the safe. Alan will deactivate the alarm and we'll all get with our lives.

TOM: That sounds good actually.

CLEM: I'm telling you Tom, plans are my specialty. Right, are you ready?

TOM: Wait, let's give it a few more minutes. Alan might still be nearby.

CLEM: Good point. Okay, let's wait a little while.

Silence.

CLEM: How accurate do you think prison films are?

TOM: What?

CLEM: Well, for a moment, I imagined myself in a prison, and I wondered what it would be like.

TOM: I think they're pretty accurate. They have people who research all of that stuff.

CLEM: Do they have those yards where all the inmates go to exercise and trade Luckies?

TOM: I'm not sure that they call them Luckies, but I think they do.

CLEM: I'd also need to learn some prison lingo, or "Peddler's French", as I believe it it's sometimes called. I could probably pick up some key phrases from the homies in my cell.

TOM: I'm sure they'll be a welcoming bunch.

CLEM: One thing I do know is that you have to be ready to hit the ground running. On your first day you have to punch someone in the face.

TOM: Really?

CLEM: It's called a chin check.

TOM: That doesn't seem like a good way to make a positive first impression.

CLEM: Well, prison isn't really about making positive first impressions, Tom. The chin check kind of sets up your stall, as it were, it lets everyone know that you won't be a candy ass.

TOM: I think I am a candy ass.

CLEM: No, you're not.

TOM: Really?

CLEM: Well, you have other strengths. Let's just leave it at that. Come on, Alan will be gone by now. Let's just get this over with.

TOM: Okay.

CLEM: And you're sure that we can't keep just a little bit of the money?

TOM: No.

CLEM: Not even a –

TOM: No!

CLEM: Fine. Now, we've got to move fast. The alarm is going to go off and it's going to be loud. But don't panic. Just get the money back in the safe and then we get out of here. Got it?

TOM: Got it.

CLEM: Here we go. Three... Two... You're sure we can't keep just a little –

TOM: No!

CLEM: Fine. Three... Two... One...

They move. The alarm is set off. CLEM and TOM spring into action, attempting to open the safe, but having problems with the two keys.

CLEM: Open it. Open it!

TOM: I can't find the right key. I can never find the right key. Why are there so many keys!

CLEM: Don't panic, Tom. Stay calm.

TOM: I hate keys!

CLEM: What's that noise?

TOM: It's my heart. I feel like it's going to explode.

CLEM: Someone's at the door.

TOM: What?

CLEM: There is someone at the door. I can hear them. Tom, we need to hide.

CLEM hides. TOM is running to a hiding place but is caught in the middle of the room, when ALAN enters and turns on the lights.

ALAN: Tom?

TOM: Alan. Hello.

ALAN: What the hell are you doing here?

TOM: ... I don't know.

CLEM pops out of her hiding place.

CLEM: The alarm went off.

ALAN: Clementine? Why are you here too?

CLEM: I was with Tom. We came to deactivate the alarm, but the code has been changed.

ALAN deactivates the alarm.

ALAN: I know. I changed it. I was here a few minutes ago.

CLEM: We were having a drink when Tom got a call to say the alarm had gone off and we came straight here. Didn't we, Tom?

TOM: ...

CLEM: Tom, say yes.

TOM: Yes.

CLEM: See?

ALAN: Right, well it's taken care of now. So, Tom, give me the keys to the safe.

TOM: ...

ALAN: Tom?

TOM: I would, Alan. You know that I would, it's just that you said, under no circumstances should I give you the keys to the safe.

ALAN: Well, I've changed my mind.

TOM: You said, "Even if I say I've changed my mind. Don't give me the keys to the safe."

ALAN: Listen to me you little twerp, give me the keys.

TOM: ... Now, I hate to sound like a broken record here, but you did say that even if you threatened me I was not to give you the keys to the safe.

ALAN grabs hold of TOM.

TOM: Oh dear.

CLEM: Let's all just calm down a little bit, shall we?

ALAN: Give me the keys.

TOM gives him the keys.

ALAN: You did the right thing. How much is in the safe?

TOM: ...

ALAN: Tom?

CLEM: ... Eight thousand. I think he said. Didn't you?

TOM: What?

CLEM: Eight thousand. Isn't that how much is *in* the safe?

TOM: Yes.

ALAN: Oh no.

ALAN doesn't bother opening the safe.

TOM: What's wrong?

ALAN: I need... Are you sure that's how much?

TOM: Well, actually...

CLEM: You told me eight thousand. You can open the safe and count it again.

ALAN: No, don't bother.

TOM: Something wrong.

ALAN: I need money.

TOM: You need money? What do you mean?

ALAN: I need two thousand.

CLEM: There is eight thousand in the safe.

ALAN: I mean two thousand more.

CLEM: So ten thousand total?

ALAN: Yes.

TOM: Why?

ALAN: That is none of your business. None of this is any of your business. You shouldn't even be here.

CLEM: You know what, Alan is right. We shouldn't even be here. Come on Tom, let's go.

They are about to leave, CLEM picks up the bag.

ALAN: Wait. Please, don't go. I need your help.

TOM: With what?

ALAN: I need ten grand or I'm going to get chopped into pieces and fed to pigs.

TOM: ... My hearing isn't always... Did you just say...

ALAN: I've lost a lot of money to some people who, well let's just say, if given the choice you would prefer not to lose money to.

CLEM: Like gangsters?

TOM: Clem! Is it gangsters?

ALAN: I don't think that is what they would call themselves, but that shoe would certainly fit. They're Estonian and they're ruthless.

TOM: So, you're in debt?

CLEM: Ironic, wouldn't you say?

ALAN: This isn't debt. Debt is a loan with a fixed rate of interest, that if leveraged correctly can help an individual build a favorable credit rating. This is owing money to people with no rules, no constitution and no independent regulatory body.

TOM: So, you were going to steal the money from the company?

ALAN: It's only stealing if you get caught.

CLEM: That's what I said.

TOM: It's not. It's stealing whether you get caught or not.

ALAN: They're going to hurt me. They're really going to hurt me.

TOM: There is eight thousand in the safe, Alan. Do you think they would take that as a partial repayment?

ALAN: I doubt it.

TOM: Why not?

ALAN: Let's just say I may have…exhausted my options.

CLEM: How did you lose it?

ALAN: …

CLEM: Alan?

ALAN: The dogs.

TOM: You spent ten thousand on a dog? You should have gone to a rescue shelter.

ALAN: I didn't buy the dogs.

CLEM: You bet on them?

ALAN: Yes.

TOM: I had no idea that you gambled.

ALAN: Yes, I gamble. I'm a gambler. I have, what I call an enjoyable hobby, but what I think is more appropriately referred to as a severe gambling addiction. I'm a ludomaniac.

CLEM: Is that what a gambling addiction is called?

TOM: Ludo, like the board game?

CLEM: Which came first I wonder?

ALAN: You two are so insensitive. I'm facing the very real possibility of having my hands chopped off and you're talking about the etymology of the word for gambling addiction. What am I going to do? I don't want to die.

CLEM: You're not going to die, Alan. Look, you're a little hot under the collar. Why don't you take yourself into the bathroom and splash a little cold water on your face, take a few deep breaths and calm down? Then you can come back out here and we'll try to figure out a plan. Plans are a bit of a specialty of mine.

ALAN: You're right. I need to get myself together.

CLEM: Exactly.

ALAN: I need to stay calm and think this through. Right.

ALAN exits.

TOM: Wow. This is getting weird. What do we do?

CLEM: About what?

TOM: We've got the money that he needs in a plastic bag. And if we don't give it to him, then he's going to get his head put in a microwave.

CLEM: Firstly, microwaves only work when the door is closed, and you couldn't close the door if someone's head was in it. And secondly, why don't we just put the money back in the safe, then he can get it and you can say you counted it wrong.

TOM: I can't say I counted it wrong.

CLEM: Why not?

TOM: Because counting is basically my job. If he finds out that I counted eight thousand instead of ten he'll sack me. Plus, he took the keys when he wanted to open the safe.

CLEM: Right. No keys. Okay.

TOM: So, now what do we do?

CLEM: We can't tell him it's his money, because he'll know we've stolen it. But we could tell him it's our money.

TOM: And then give it to him. Yes.

CLEM: No.

TOM: No, what?

CLEM: We don't give it to him.

TOM: But you just said.

CLEM: We *lend* it to him.

TOM: What?

CLEM: We lend it to him, like he lends to other people.

TOM: But it's his money.

CLEM: No, it isn't. We stole it from him. It's ours now. It's in our bag.

TOM: We can't do that.

CLEM: We can. And we will. He's desperate for money and he's about to know what that's like.

TOM: No, we will just give it to him.

CLEM: Why should we give it to him? He wouldn't give it to either of us?

TOM: He's in trouble.

CLEM: So are we and we didn't get into it by betting on the dogs.

TOM: I think we should just help him out.

CLEM: No, we shouldn't. This is his comeuppance.

TOM: What is?

CLEM: This. He's a bad man, Tom. He's a gambling addict and he drinks whisky at work. Plus, he sacked me about five hours ago, so this is his comeuppance.

TOM: People don't get their comeuppance in real life, Clem. That's just something that happens in films, so that we can all feel better about getting screwed over all the time.

CLEM: Alan is about to learn the consequences of his behavior.

TOM: No, he isn't Clem, he's about to get his face smashed in by a bunch of Etonians.

CLEM: They're Estonians, Tom. They aren't Etonians.

TOM: What's the difference?

CLEM: Well, these Estonians make money through unethical means, and Etonians mostly work in finance.

TOM: Wherever they're from, they are obviously capable of violence and I won't be responsible for Alan getting his testicles put in the microwave.

CLEM: What is it with you and microwaves?

TOM: I don't know. I must be hungry. I didn't eat dinner.

CLEM: Alan has forced us into a corner and now we're going to force him into one.

TOM: I'm not. This cycle of people leaning on each other, extorting each other without guilt or shame to make a little extra money has to stop.

CLEM: But why does it have to stop with us?

TOM: Because we're good people.

ALAN enters.

ALAN: Well, that didn't help at all.

TOM: We can help you, Alan.

ALAN: Unless you've got a lot of money or a sub machine gun, I don't think you can.

TOM: We can give you the two thousand.

ALAN: What?

CLEM: But it's going to come with some serious conditions.

TOM: No, it isn't.

CLEM: Is.

TOM: Isn't.

CLEM: Is.

TOM: Isn't.

ALAN: Can someone please tell me what is going on here?

CLEM: We're going to lend you money the way you lend other people money.

ALAN: Me? I don't lend anybody money. It's the company that I work for.

CLEM: How is that not you?

ALAN: I'm a branch manager. I have about as much to do with the running of this place as a train driver has with what route his train takes.

CLEM: I'm sure you've argued many times to have the interest rates lowered, haven't you?

ALAN: That isn't the way it works.

CLEM: So, how does it work? You just do as you're told and swallow all your principles.

ALAN: Principles? I can't afford principles.

CLEM: So, you're perfectly fine with the way this company operates?

ALAN: I wouldn't say I was fine with it entirely, but I have to make a living. If I ever tried to speak out against any of this I could lose my job. And I can't afford to lose my job, I've got a ferocious gambling habit to feed.

CLEM: And you think I could afford to lose mine?

ALAN: No, but that's the way it works. Life is like a greyhound race. You have to do everything that you can to stay near the front. If someone falls behind leave them. If someone gets injured it's bad luck. You have to take care of yourself, and only yourself. You're young. You haven't been running for very long and you're at the back of the pack. So, you have two choices you can either get in the race and try to get to the front, or you can complain that you're in a race and you'll always be near the back.

CLEM: Is that really how it is?

ALAN: That's the system that we live in. I didn't invent it, I don't particularly like it, but that's the way it is and that is the way it is going to be for a while. So accept it and get into it, or don't accept and suffer. Your choice.

CLEM: … You'll pay us back. Double.

ALAN: Double? You're worse than the gangsters.

TOM: No, we're not. We would never put your…

CLEM: Tom, if you say anything about a body part going in a microwave I'm going to lose my shit.

TOM: Sorry.

ALAN: Double?

CLEM: What can I say, Alan, life is a greyhound race. Well, I'm getting ahead.

TOM: Stop it, Clem. Don't let it do this to you. Alan, we'll give you the money. You're in trouble and you need help, so we're going to give it to you.

TOM moves towards the bag with the money.

CLEM: Wait!

TOM: No, Clem.

CLEM: Yes. Wait, we have to go back to our houses.

TOM: Why?

CLEM: Because that's where we keep our money. Isn't it, Tom? We certainly don't have it here, do we?

TOM: Oh. That's right. We'll have to go back to our houses to get the money.

ALAN: That's okay.

TOM: Because that's where we keep our money.

ALAN: Of course it is.

TOM: We certainly don't have it here.

ALAN: You're just repeating everything that she said.

TOM: So, I'll just get my bag, which contains a few grocery items that we earlier purchased from a local convenience store.

CLEM: That's why they're in a plastic bag.

ALAN: Those things wreak havoc with the oceans.

CLEM: They do, don't they?

TOM: And we'll go home and get the money.

ALAN: Good idea. I'm very grateful to you both for helping me out. Now, let's get on with it and get this whole thing over with.

ALAN begins setting the alarm.

ALARM: Incorrect code entered.

ALAN: This alarm is infuriating. Can't we turn off the voice or something?

CLEM: I'll take a look.

ALAN: I really appreciate this, Tom. Maybe, when all this is over, you and I can sit down and discuss a few more days unpaid leave. And Clementine, as soon as things pick up around here, you'll be my first phone call.

CLEM: I've turned the voice settings to "Essential warnings only".

ALAN: Good. Thanks. And thank you again for helping me out. I feel much better now.

ALAN sets the alarm and they walk out the door. The door is barely closed when ALAN pushes them back into the room with urgency.

ALAN: Get back inside. Get in. Shut the door.

CLEM: Why?

TOM: What's going on?

ALAN locks the door.

ALAN: It's the Estonians. They're here.

TOM: They're outside?

ALAN: Yes, the two Range Rovers that just turned into the street, that's them.

TOM: What are they doing here?

ALAN: They've come for their money.

CLEM: They must have followed you.

ALAN: What am I going to do? We don't have the money yet?

TOM seems about to take the money out of the bag. CLEM grabs it before he can. ALAN's gaze is firmly locked outside the window.

TOM: Yes, we do.

CLEM: No, we don't.

TOM: Yes, we do.

CLEM: Tom, we don't.

ALAN: They've stopped outside.

CLEM: We need to go and get it.

TOM: No, we don't.

TOM and CLEM are wrestling with the bag.

ALAN: It's them. It's definitely them.

ALARM: Alarm activated.

ALAN, CLEM and TOM freeze in the middle of the room.

SCENE FOUR

3:00pm. Earlier that day. TOM is alone and is fiddling with the alarm.

ALARM: Would you like to return to the main menu?

TOM: No, I want to go to sensitivity settings.

ALARM: Would you like to change the alarm tone?

TOM: No, I already told you, I want to go to sensitivity settings.

ALARM: Would you like to change the language?

TOM: You're just not going to play ball, are you?

ALAN enters. He carries a briefcase tightly.

TOM: There you are, Alan. It's almost three o'clock. Where have you been?

ALAN: Don't ask.

ALAN opens his briefcase and takes out lots of cash.

ALAN: Run this through, Tom. No questions asked.

TOM: Where is it from?

ALAN: Didn't I just say no questions asked?

TOM: I just need to know who it is from, so I can credit it to their account.

ALAN: It's all in the form.

TOM walks over to the desk and picks up the form.

TOM: Mrs. Sally Flash.

TOM looks at the money inside the briefcase.

TOM: Wow. Alan, this is a lot of money. Is this all one loan?

ALAN: Listen Tom, I really just need you not to ask about this. I don't have time for questions, I've been… Yes, this person borrowed this money from us. And now they have to return it, quickly, before anyone, I mean before… Listen, just clear their account and put the money in the safe.

TOM: Okay.

TOM moves to his desk.

ALAN: Where is Clem?

TOM: Bathroom.

MERYL enters.

MERYL: Hello again.

ALAN: Meryl, shit.

MERYL: Hello is fine.

ALAN: I didn't think you'd be…is it three? Damn, it is.

MERYL: Just came to make sure we were…on schedule. So, are we Alan?

ALAN: No, I haven't… I was about to.

CLEM enters.

CLEM: Hey, Alan.

ALAN: Oh hi, Clem…

ALAN and MERYL smile an awkward smile. CLEM can sense the strangeness of it, and goes back to her desk. TOM begins counting the money.

MERYL: *(To ALAN.)* Just remember what I told you. Capitalism and inevitability, hard choices. That's it. Short and sweet.

ALAN: Right.

MERYL: It worked on you, didn't it?

ALAN: Sure did.

MERYL: It works on everyone.

ALAN: Okay. Right, here goes. Clementine?

CLEM: What?

ALAN: There's something I need to talk to you about.

CLEM: Okay.

ALAN: Well, as you know the government is about to renew the regulatory regulations that our business is…regulated by.

CLEM: Yes.

ALAN: Honestly Clem, I've got to tell you, we're a business on a small high street. We make a small amount of money off some small people and their relatives. That's nothing compared to some people in the world. Oh, I get it. We're in the Bible. And Shakespeare. But just because we don't swap mortgages they get away with it. Anyway, the regulations could be hard on us.

CLEM: Okay.

ALAN: There could be branch closures, cutbacks. Who knows? My old friend Trevor Wynyard might even declare the company bankrupt.

CLEM: He'd do that?

MERYL is shaking her head at ALAN.

ALAN: No, no, no. He mentioned something off hand, but I'm pretty sure he was joking. Don't you worry about the big boy shit, Clem. Trying to regulate capitalism is like a river full of tennis balls.

MERYL's head falls into her hands.

CLEM: Why?

ALAN: … Just… Very… Very unusual. But in the end, doesn't it still flow?

MERYL: Oh, for God's sake, Alan! Clem, I'm afraid I've got some bad news. In an effort to cut company running costs in anticipation of the new industry regulations, we're going to have to let you go.

CLEM: … What?

MERYL: The business is going through some changes and unfortunately we can no longer afford to keep you on. We're very sorry. But, don't worry, you're young, you'll have plenty of other chances. If you need us in future, we'd be happy to provide you with an excellent reference.

CLEM: … That's it?

MERYL: Yes, that's it.

CLEM: … I just go home now?

MERYL: You can go anywhere that you want to.

CLEM: Okay. Well… That's…okay…fine. I hated working here anyway. I hate what this company does. I think it's evil and predatory, and I'm glad I won't have to face it anymore. Maybe I'll finally get a job that I don't feel like I have to wash off at the end of the day. Alan, Meryl, I hope the new regulations crush this business into the ground, and both of you along with it. See you, Tom.

CLEM leaves.

MERYL: See, easy. Now…

MERYL points to TOM, who is trying not to look up.

ALAN: Tom?

TOM: Yes?

ALAN: … Meryl needs to talk to you, too.

TOM: Oh no. Please, don't. I really can't afford to –

MERYL: No, Tom, Tom, stop. You're not losing your job.

TOM: Oh, thank goodness.

MERYL: But we are cutting your salary.

TOM: … Okay.

MERYL: That's okay?

TOM: Well, no, but it's better than losing my job altogether.

MERYL: That's the spirit, Tom. Excellent. Well, my work here is done.

MERYL begins heading towards the door.

MERYL: I'll be back at nine o'clock tomorrow, Alan and we'll have a good long look at your accounts.

ALAN: Oh God.

MERYL: What did you say?

ALAN: I said, okay. Okay. See you tomorrow.

TOM: Bye, Meryl.

MERYL exits. TOM returns to counting the money. ALAN moves to his desk and sneakily takes a guzzle of his whisky.

ALAN: Listen Tom, I'm sorry about all this. Sometimes in business, you have to make hard choices.

TOM: It's fine. It's okay. It's just that I could really have used that money.

ALAN: I know. Times are hard.

TOM: They're certainly not easy. I'm working just about every hour I've got and can't afford to pay the rent on the house that I'm never at because I'm so busy working to not afford it.

ALAN: … Listen, I'll throw you a bone. This new alarm system is driving me mad. This morning I had to drive into work at four o'clock to reset it. I have no idea what set it off, but I don't want to come all the way here every time it happens. So, how about I add it to your duties?

TOM: Okay.

ALAN: If the alarm goes off, it automatically contacts you, you come to the shop and reset it. You only live nearby, so it will be easier for you to get here. And I'll pay you for your time.

TOM: That's great. That will really help me out.

ALAN: Take my keys for now, and I'll get you a new set cut.

ALAN gives TOM the keys.

ALAN: The code is 1-4-9-3, no it isn't. Its 1-9-4-3. No, it is 1-4-9-3. I always forget. Now, if you get it wrong twice, you'll have to change the code. If you change it make sure you write down what you change it to, okay?

TOM: Yes. I think.

ALAN: Why don't you try it out to make sure it's in your head?

TOM goes to the alarm to test the code.

ALAN: *(About the money on the desk.)* It's a funny thing money. Actually, it's not funny at all, it's absolutely horrible. I don't know why I said it was funny. I hate it.

ALAN picks up a bundle of the money and looks at it with a strange fascination.

ALAN: Tom, I have a…

TOM: A what?

ALAN: Just keep that away from me, okay? I'm going to just go home. You can lock up when you're done. The safe keys are on there as well. Count the money and stick it in there.

TOM: Don't you want to take it to the bank?

ALAN: No. Not tonight. I'll do it tomorrow.

TOM: Will it be alright in the safe overnight?

ALAN: It will be fine.

TOM: Okay.

ALAN: Under no circumstances give me the keys to the safe. Is that clear?

TOM: Yes.

ALAN: If I tell you that I've changed my mind, ignore me. Even if I threaten you, do not give me the keys to the safe. Is all of this going in?

TOM: Yes.

ALARM: Alarm settings.

TOM: Oh, finally!

TOM moves to the alarm.

ALAN: I hate that alarm.

TOM: If I can just turn the sensitivity settings down a little, that should stop it from going off so often. You go, I'll take care of everything here.

ALAN: I will. I should.

ALAN is tempted by the money sitting on the desk. He slowly walks to it. TOM keeps his focus on the alarm.

TOM: I think this is sensitivity.

ALAN picks up one of the bundles of money and puts it in his pocket. He turns and goes to walk out the door.

ALARM: La langue a change.

TOM: No, that's not it.

At the door ALAN stops. He turns and returns to the desk.

ALARM: Sprache ändern.

TOM: No.

ALAN puts the money back.

ALARM: Linguaggio è cambiato.

ALAN picks the money up again.

TOM: I don't know what I'm doing here.

ALAN puts the money back.

ALARM: Språket endret

TOM: You'd think this would be easy.

ALAN picks the money up.

ALARM: Lenguaje cambió

TOM: No, that's not right.

ALAN puts the money down.

ALARM: Language changed.

ALAN: *(Shouted.)* Oh for God's sake!

TOM: Sorry Alan, I'm trying my best.

ALAN: No, Tom, it isn't you… It's the alarm. Why do they make these things so complicated? Why does everything have to be so complicated?

TOM: I don't know, Alan. I find myself asking that question a lot.

ALAN walks away.

ALAN: I'm going home. Count the money, put it in the safe, and don't give me the keys under any circumstances.

TOM: I'm sure that's not going to come up.

ALAN: Just don't.

TOM: Okay.

ALAN leaves. TOM goes back to the alarm. After a moment, ALAN enters.

ALAN: Forgot my…something…wallet.

TOM doesn't turn around. ALAN takes money from the briefcase and walks straight back out.

TOM: Bye, Alan. Have a good night.

ALAN: I almost certainly will not.

SCENE FIVE

1:00am. ALAN, TOM and CLEM are as they were at the end of scene three.

ALAN: *(Without moving his mouth.)* Will it set the alarm off if I move my mouth?

TOM: No.

CLEM: Perfectly valid question though.

ALAN: What do we do now?

CLEM: Nothing.

ALAN: Nothing? The Estonians will be outside any second and if any of us moves a muscle we'll set the alarm off.

CLEM: So, we stay still. If there is anyone out there, let's hope they didn't see us, and if they didn't see us then they would have no reason to suspect anyone is in here. Phase Two: We wait until they leave. Phase Three: We move and set the alarm off. Phase Four: You deactivate the alarm. And Phase Five: We get out of here as fast as we can.

ALAN: That's a really good plan, actually.

CLEM: Thank you. Plans are a specialty of mine.

TOM: And what if they did see us?

CLEM: ... They probably didn't.

TOM: But if they did.

CLEM: I really doubt they did.

TOM: I know, but if they did.

CLEM: We were hardly out the door. Just keep calm and don't move a muscle, exactly like last time.

ALAN: Last time? What do you mean last time?

CLEM: ... Oh, I just meant the last time Tom felt a little flustered. I always remind him to stay calm and not move a muscle. It helps him.

TOM: I think they saw us.

ALAN: If they did it's every man for himself.

CLEM: Every person for themselves, would be more appropriate, but I'm pretty sure they didn't see us. They'd only just turned the corner. And this is, of course, even assuming that it was them. A lot of people drive black Range Rovers.

TOM: There were two in convoy.

CLEM: A lot of people drive two black Range Rovers in convoy.

TOM: Like who?

CLEM: Royalty, diplomats, it's incredibly common. We're not going to know anything more by playing guessing games. Let's just wait and see.

ALAN: Fine.

TOM: Fine.

Silence.

CLEM: Are the gangsters funny?

ALAN: Funny?

CLEM: Yes. Do they exchange, you know, wit and banter? Or discuss their curious philosophies on life with a surprisingly diverse vocabulary?

ALAN: No.

CLEM: Not even the ones lower down the pecking order?

ALAN: No.

CLEM: I'm really surprised. You'd have thought they would be charming like in the movies.

ALAN: They're just horrible people. They prey on the weak and the needy and the desperate.

CLEM: It's funny hearing you say that, Alan.

ALAN: Listen, this might not be the most ethical profession in the world, but at least we're better than gangsters.

CLEM: Why? Because we have a shop and a duck for a mascot?

ALAN: Amongst other reasons, yes. We're an important part of society. We're good. We're like a charity.

CLEM: Is that what you tell yourself to help you sleep at night?

ALAN: No. I prefer single malt whisky. At least I did. But I had to downgrade to blended whisky. Now, I'm on to mouthwash over ice.

TOM: Why don't you get help, Alan?

ALAN: Because if I move I'll set the alarm off.

TOM: Not now. I mean…for your…you know, in your life.

ALAN: I've tried to get help. I've gone to meetings, I've done counseling but sooner or later I always end up back here.

Well, not exactly here, but you get what I mean. Trust me, I've tried.

CLEM: Well, maybe you should try harder.

ALAN: You don't know what you're talking about.

CLEM: Don't I?

ALAN: No, you don't. If you think it's easy to resist this kind of temptation then you're wrong. I turn on the television and I see gambling adverts, I walk down the street and I see betting shops, I get emails sent to my account, flyers through my door, if I don't show up at the bookmakers for a few days they practically send someone to my house with a can of cider and a roulette wheel. Honestly, it's like a recovering food addict living in the birthday cake aisle. Have you ever been to a greyhound race?

TOM: No.

CLEM: Definitely not.

ALAN: You will never find a stranger place. Take earlier tonight. So, I placed my bet, ironically on a dog called Fast Freddie, who really should have been named Limping, Slow, Soon to be Euthanized Freddie, but that's another story. I walk back through the people slurping beer and shoving pies into their face, and I take a seat in the stands. Suddenly, just before the hare is released I have a moment of clarity, like a man waking up from a nightmare and I think to myself, what the hell am I doing? I've just bet money on one dog running faster than other dogs and nobody, at any point, tried to stop me. In fact, all I ever got from anyone was encouragement. By the time I snap out of it, the dogs are halfway around the track and Fast Freddie drops back to last place, and they cross the finish line. My betting slip falls down to the floor and I run from the stadium. I'm driving back here, passing shops, restaurants, billboards, I'm running red lights and swerving around corners, and I realize why no one cares. It's because there is an incredibly fine line between being an addict and being a good customer, and good customers are what we want. We're all trying to make good customers of each other. We're trying to get each other hooked on whatever it is that we're selling, so that we'll irrationally keep hitting the buy button.

Silence.

ALAN: We live in a society that pays very little money, encourages people to spend even more and blames them when they do.

Silence.

ALAN: Might as well get it all out on the table. Even if I make it through tonight, I'm in trouble.

TOM: Why?

ALAN: Well, starting tomorrow, Meryl is going to begin going over our books. When she does, she will discover that not everything is as it should be. In fact, almost nothing is as it should be. I'll go down for fraud or embezzlement or theft. I suppose tonight is what they call a tipping point for me. I'm either going to wind up dead or in prison.

TOM: I don't understand.

ALAN: Tom – I'm Sally Flash.

TOM: … On the weekends?

ALAN: No, Mrs. Sally Flash.

CLEM: What's he talking about?

TOM: You took out that loan?

ALAN: Yes, and many others.

CLEM: What loan?

TOM: The loan that he paid back today. You took it out under a false name? Surely that's illegal.

ALAN: Yes, it is. I've been taking out loans under false names and bypassing the usual security checks for months. With new regulations coming in, we're going to be under a lot more scrutiny so I had to find a way to pay them all back.

TOM: Then you lost the gangster's money so you were going to steal from the company to pay them back?

ALAN: Yes.

TOM: Vicious circle, isn't it?

CLEM: So, this is all because of you?

ALAN: Well...maybe not all.

CLEM: We have struggled so much. Tom can barely afford to pay his rent, I've got bills piling up and you're telling us the reason I lost my job and Tom got a pay cut is because you like playing the dogs?

ALAN: I was about to say I'm sorry.

CLEM: What is that going to do?

TOM: Clementine?

CLEM: You want to say sorry so that we'll forgive you?

TOM: Clementine?

CLEM: Well, we're not going to. You're pathetic, you're a weak, cowardly thief. We should set off this alarm and hand you over to gangsters. Watch them cut you into pieces and feed you to their cats.

TOM: Clementine, stop it.

CLEM: No, I won't stop it, Tom. Why don't you ever take my side?

TOM: I'm not taking anyone's side, but shouting at Alan isn't going to help.

CLEM: Well, constantly lying down and letting people walk all over you isn't either.

TOM: Can we please just focus on the situation? Things are already bad enough as it is, we don't need to make them any worse.

There is a loud smashing sound, someone trying to break through the back door.

CLEM: What is that?

ALAN: The back door.

TOM: Someone is trying to break in.

The alarm sounds.

ALARM: Intruder alert! Intruder alert!

ALAN: I'm a dead man.

TOM: Hide!

TOM, CLEM and ALAN all hide around the shop.

SCENE SIX

4:30pm. Earlier that day. TOM is at his desk counting money. CLEM enters.

TOM: Clem, what are you doing back here? I thought you'd gone home.

CLEM: Don't worry, I'm not here to set the place on fire.

TOM: Well, that's certainly good news. If you're looking for Alan he left about half an hour ago.

CLEM: I just forgot my...

She sees the money.

CLEM: What's that?

TOM: Oh, it's a loan repayment. Alan brought it in. Clem, I'm sorry about you losing your job.

CLEM: That's okay.

TOM: If it makes you feel any better, I got a pay cut, too.

CLEM: It's a funny thing money.

TOM: I really don't think it is.

CLEM: That's all it is. Those little slips of paper, but they have so much power. It doesn't make sense.

TOM: Well, I suppose if you're talking abstractly, then no, perhaps it doesn't make sense.

CLEM: ... Tom?

TOM: Yes.

CLEM: Alan brought this in?

TOM: Yes.

CLEM: Did anyone else see him?

TOM: I don't think so.

CLEM: ... We should take it.

TOM: What?

CLEM: That. We should take it.

TOM: We can't do that.

CLEM: Yes, we can. It's cash and you haven't added it to the accounts yet. The only people who know it is here are you, me and Alan. How could anyone prove it?

TOM: Are you being serious?

CLEM: Come on, Tom, think about what this business has taken from us. Well, we can take something back.

CLEM grabs the wad of cash.

TOM: No! No, we can't just take money from the shop.

CLEM: You're saying we need to make it look like an outside job?

TOM: That's not what I'm saying at all.

CLEM: You're right. We break in in the middle of the night. We leave no trace. Then why would they suspect us?

TOM: Clem, we can't steal from the company.

CLEM: Why not?

TOM: Because it isn't ethical.

CLEM: None of this is ethical, Tom. None of it. This business, any business, the lending, the borrowing, the whole fucking financial system. None of it is even remotely near ethical. Why should it expect us to act ethically in return?

Silence.

TOM: How would we do it?

SCENE SEVEN

1:30am. As they were at the end of scene five. ALAN, TOM and CLEM are panicking and searching for hiding spots.

MERYL, dressed all in black, enters. She holds a hammer in one hand, which she used to break open the back door. She slowly walks to the alarm control panel, investigates it briefly, then smashes it. The alarm sound stops.

ALARM: *(Slurred.)* Control panel compromised.

MERYL turns back, into the room. ALAN stands.

ALAN: Please! Don't do this. I don't want to die. Please, I'm begging you. Please.

MERYL: … Alan?

ALAN: I haven't got all your money, I've got some of it, part of it. Most of it. Please, don't kill me, I'm too young to die.

Well, I suppose that's not true, I'm probably of a dying age, but that doesn't mean I'm ready.

MERYL takes off her mask.

MERYL: Alan? What are you doing here?

ALAN: Meryl?

MERYL: It's one thirty in the morning. Alan, do you sleep at the shop?

ALAN: No, I don't. I thought you were… Why did you come in through the back door?

MERYL: There are two black Range Rovers parked out front. I thought they might be Wynyard's security.

ALAN: Why would Wynyard's security be here?

MERYL: We're finished, Alan. It's over. The whole ball game. The whole shenanigan. The music has stopped and all of the guests have…

ALAN: Meryl, I know you like a good metaphor, but will you please just tell me what is going on?

MERYL: Wynyard has liquidated the business. The Debt Duck is officially dead. The new regulations would have killed it, so he put it out of its misery. And you and I are both out of the job.

ALAN: You said he'd never do that.

MERYL: I thought he was joking.

ALAN: And what happened to him consulting you and you consulting me?

MERYL: He said a lot of things, but they were all lies.
How could that bastard betray me like this? I thought I was in the club. What am I going to do now?

ALAN: What am I going to do now?

TOM stands.

TOM: What am I going to do now?

MERYL: Tom! What are you doing here? *(To ALAN.)* Does he sleep at the shop?

TOM: The alarm went off. I came to deactivate it.

MERYL: Anything else I should know about?

CLEM stands.

CLEM: While we're all getting out in the open.

MERYL: Anyone else?

ALAN: That's it.

ALARM: Control panel compromised.

ALAN: And the alarm, if she counts.

MERYL: *(To TOM.)* You heard?

TOM: Yes.

MERYL: I'm sorry, Tom.

TOM: That's alright.

MERYL: But don't worry, you're young enough, you'll have other chances.

ALAN: I still don't understand what you're doing here, Meryl?

MERYL: I've just lost my job, Alan. I'm doing what every responsible executive would do in my situation

ALAN: You're cleaning out the safe?

MERYL: Exactly.

TOM: What is wrong with everyone tonight?

MERYL: Why shouldn't I?

TOM: Because it's stealing.

MERYL: It's only stealing if you get caught.

TOM: Why does everyone keep saying that!

MERYL: Listen, Tom, if you think I can afford to think about what is right and what is not right now, then you clearly don't understand my mortgage. It's like a monster that eats everything I have and still demands more.

CLEM: And you think stealing a few thousand from the safe is going to help?

MERYL: Well, it definitely isn't going to hurt.

ALAN: I'm the manager of this branch, if anyone is going to steal from it, it should be me.

MERYL: Alan, you're the worst manager I've ever seen. You're lucky you've made it this far.

ALAN: I'll have you know, I work very hard here.

CLEM: Ha!

MERYL: Your shop is in the middle of skid row and you couldn't sell payday loans, Alan. You've spent years in a barrel full of tits and all you've done is suck your thumb.

ALAN: You swan in here in your trouser suit at the end of every quarter and tell me how to do my job, but you don't know what it's like going face to face with these people. Why don't you try running a branch for a change? The only thing you know how to run is your mouth.

CLEM: Running a branch? Is that what you've been doing?

ALAN: Stay out of this, Clementine.

CLEM: By dipping your fingers into the profits and blowing them at the dog track?

MERYL: What is she talking about?

ALAN: I said stay out of this.

CLEM: Okay Alan, or should I say Sally?

ALAN: Shut up Clementine!

MERYL: What's she talking about? Dipping into the profits?

ALAN: Nothing.

CLEM: Alan has been stealing from the business to fund a gambling habit, which now has him in debt to a gang of loan sharks who are waiting outside and Alan doesn't have the money to pay them back.

MERYL: ... Remember that expression, something about throwing your problems in a pile and wishing for your own. Well, is that ever true? Greyhounds, gambling, gangsters? I thought you were just bad at your job.

ALAN: I have had some problems with gambling, but it's nothing that I can't handle.

MERYL: So the Range Rovers aren't Wynyard's men?

CLEM: They're the gangsters.

MERYL looks out the window.

MERYL: I've never really had anything to do with gangsters. Are they funny like in the movies?

CLEM: Apparently not.

MERYL: That's a shame.

ALAN: Oh yeah, it's a real shame that the gangsters here to kill me don't conform to their stereotypes. Maybe while they're pulling out my fingernails I'll ask them if they know any knock-knock jokes.

MERYL: I wonder if they'd hire me. I don't know what hench means, and I'm not a man, but if they needed a regional manager I could be of some use.

ALAN: You wouldn't like it, their interest rates are lower than ours and they don't have a pension scheme.

MERYL: Well, they should get one and a mascot, too. Desperate people will still need money. Where do you think they're going to go to get it?

CLEM: You're just feeling bitter because you lost.

MERYL: Lost? Oh, please, shutting down one payday lender and declaring it a victory is like killing a mole and declaring your lawn safe. There's more. There's thousands more lurking under the surface waiting to rear their heads.

CLEM: So, what's the solution since you seem to know everything?

MERYL: I don't know, my husband does the gardening.

CLEM: Well, you'll have plenty of time to help him now that you're unemployed and there will be one less company fleecing people on the high street, one less problem for a lot of people to worry about.

MERYL: We're not the problem, we were never the problem. The problem isn't that there are people who prey upon the weak, the problem is that they're allowed to get that weak in the first place.

Silence.

MERYL: Anyway, we're wasting time. How much is in the safe?

TOM: Ten thousand.

CLEM: Eight thousand.

MERYL: *(To CLEM.)* And how much is in your plastic bag?

CLEM looks at the bag, surprised that she saw it.

CLEM: Nothing.

MERYL: I'm guessing two thousand.

TOM: Yes.

CLEM: No.

TOM: Yes. It's the two thousand that we were going to steal.

ALAN: How dare you!

TOM: That we were going to give to you.

ALAN: Oh, well done. Wait a minute, you were going to lend me my own money?

MERYL: That you stole that from the company?

ALAN: Listen, we don't have all night to sit around and talk about this, we need to make a decision. What do we do with the money?

CLEM: I think the best thing to do is divide the eight thousand four ways and carry on with our lives.

ALAN: There's ten thousand.

CLEM: No, there is eight thousand.

ALAN: What about that two thousand?

CLEM: That's ours. We've already stolen it.

MERYL: That doesn't make it yours.

CLEM: It's in our bag.

MERYL: Your plastic bag. You know they're very bad for the oceans?

CLEM: The way I see it. We were all planning on stealing the ten thousand. But we got here first and stole two thousand. That two thousand is now ours. The eight thousand in the safe is what we're now talking about, and since no one has stolen that yet, we all have equal claim to it.

MERYL: There is ten thousand. Clementine, you've taken two thousand out of the safe, but you haven't yet taken it out of the shop. Therefore your theft is not complete, it's pending, and so is unrecognised. We're not talking about the money that remains in the safe, we're talking about the money that remains in the business, and the two thousand in that bag is still in the business. So, let's do the right thing, and divide the money based on seniority. That means that I take a larger stake, Alan slightly smaller than that, and Tom slightly smaller than that. Okay?

CLEM: I deserve some, too.

MERYL: This is employee compensation, Clementine. You don't work here anymore.

CLEM: None of us work here. The business is finished. There is no here anymore.

ALAN: I agree with, Meryl.

CLEM: Well, I agree with me. We should get it all, we were here first.

MERYL: I should get it first, because I'm more senior.

ALAN: I should get it first because I'm about to get the shit kicked out of me.

CLEM: But that's your fault.

MERYL: She's right Alan, your problem is entirely self-inflicted, so I'm not sure you should get anything.

TOM: Stop it.

ALAN: You had no choice but to buy a big house did you?

MERYL: That's different.

ALAN: It always is.

TOM: Stop it.

MERYL: Look, I outrank all of you, so stop your blabbing and give me the money.

CLEM: You're not getting it, Meryl.

ALAN: You were the last here, you hardly have a claim at all.

TOM: Stop it!

Silence.

TOM: Look at us. We're blaming each other as though any of us has had anything to do with each other's problem? And while we fight for the scraps, Trevor Wynyard gets away scot-free. Why is nobody fighting with him? We're not each other's enemies. We're the same, and if we don't start helping each other then we're all finished.

Silence.

TOM: We're all caught in this, one way or another, but none of our problems gets any better, by making someone else's worse. I don't want the money, not if it is going to mean comprising who I am. I'm sorry, you're all good people, you deserve better than this.

TOM walks out the door.

CLEM: He's right. We shouldn't be fighting amongst ourselves. We're all in the same boat, we should be helping each other.

MERYL: Why don't we?

CLEM: Because we don't.

CLEM walks towards the door, TOM enters quickly.

TOM: Get back inside. It's the police.

ALARM: Control panel compromised.

TOM ushers them all back inside the shop and shuts the door.

CLEM: The police?

TOM: I saw two cars at the top of the street heading this way.

ALARM: Five.

ALAN: At least that will scare the Estonians off.

CLEM: Alan?

ALAN: I'm just saying, every cloud.

ALARM: Eight.

MERYL: If they find us here in the middle of night with the back door broken in, the alarm smashed to smithereens and an empty safe, we're all going down.

CLEM: How did they find out?

TOM: The alarm probably contacts them if it gets tampered with.

ALAN: I hate that alarm.

ALARM: Three.

ALAN: Oh shut up!

TOM: Clem, what do we do?

CLEM: Okay. Phase One –

ALAN: There's no time for that!

MERYL: There's nothing we can do.

TOM: Lock the door.

ALAN does.

ALARM: Nine.

ALAN: The back door! We could make a run for it.

MERYL: Then that will make us look guilty.

TOM: We are guilty!

ALARM: Two.

CLEM: We've got to stop getting trapped like this.

ALAN: There they are.

ALARM: One. Alarm activated.

The four freeze in different positions on the stage.

MERYL: Will…it…set…the…alarm…off…if… I…move…
my…mouth?

Alan/Clem/TOM: No!

THE END.